Hom Bluegrass

A Guide to Making People Happy with Music

by

Anni Beach, Band Leader

with

Jam Pak Blues 'N' Grass Neighborhood Band

Jam Pak Sunflower Publishing

Chandler, Arizona

Home Grown Bluegrass

is dedicated to the memory of

Vincent Collin Beach, the Father of

Jam Pak,

my Rock and Hero,

whose unfailing support and finances
made Jam Pak

possible from the first glimmer of the
vision.

Contents

Preface

When asked to describe Jam Pak, most of us that have been a part of it often chuckle. How do you describe to someone a culture, a way of life, or the deeply-ingrained lessons instilled in us?

Jam Pak is a band founded out of love of music and community. I tell people that the group meets twice a week in the living room of Anni Beach to learn bluegrass music. The house is filled with pictures, relics, books, and music. Banjos, guitars, violins, mandolins, and other instruments line the walls of the house, waiting to be grabbed by a young musician.

The members of Jam Pak come here to practice their music, teaching and learning from one another. The demographics of the band are significant. Jam Pak consists of members from all over the US, Mexico, Africa, Europe, and Asia. This diversity is a testament to the power of music and its ability to bring together people from different cultures and backgrounds.

A typical Tuesday consists of band rehearsal. The time outside of the practice schedule includes eating together, sharing stories from the school day, helping one another with homework, and jamming. The band travels around the state and Southwest performing and teaching. Multiple smaller bands within the group practice together after the joint rehearsal.

This brief overview usually gives people an idea of the mission of Jam Pak but it fails to communicate the intricate level of community that serves as the foundation of the band. This requires a more in-depth examination of the internal workings of Jam Pak. I hope that the story that follows will shed light on the aspects of Jam Pak that have changed my life.

I came to Jam Pak at age 12 as a classically-trained violinist seeking to expand into other styles. My Mom had discovered Jam Pak online after a Google search. I was used to the typical orchestra setup with music stands, perfect postures, and sheet music. I walked in to the practice space to find 25 other children, many younger than me, strumming along to bluegrass tunes. The entire living room was packed with chairs, people, and instruments. There was no sheet music or lyrics in sight and yet they all managed to sing and play song after song. Mrs. Beach stood proudly at the front of the room leading them. After trying to figure out the "secret" that allowed them to play by ear, I became overwhelmed and left the rehearsal in tears. Most of the group assumed that was the last they'd see of me. With the encouragement of my private lesson classical teacher, I decided to give it another try. There was something different about this group of musicians. I showed up the very next week.

I found a community that was eager to teach me the music and show me the "secrets" of learning by ear. I found a community that showed up to my school plays and performances to show their support. I found a group of people that eagerly pushed me out of my comfort zone. I found a group of friends that was present for my high school and college graduation, yelling with signs and noise makers. I found band members that I got to travel the country and the world with. All of these things were made possible by the love and teachings of Anni Beach.

She instilled in us a love of music, community, and friendship. From the moment we arrived for rehearsal on Tuesdays, we were expected to be our best. There were no rules or punishments. There was no strict code of conduct that made all 25 of us behave. We were all there because we loved to make this kind of music- from the youngest children to the adults. We loved the sound that we produced, and we loved to make others happy with our music. This is the driving force that kept us coming back each week, each month, each year. We saw the value in one another through music. We were taught that each member of the band played a crucial role in making the band sound great. Seeing value in our fellow band members as human beings was not a far stretch beyond that.

During my 12 years in Jam Pak, I have learned too many lessons to count. I started as a band member. The older, more experienced kids taught me fiddle tunes and taught me the words to the songs. I transitioned into the role of a teacher, where I taught fiddle tunes and the words to younger members. This led to a mentorship role where I took on the duties of "Camp Mom" when we traveled. I became inspired to learn clawhammer banjo and began learning to play oldtime music. Being a part of a strong community opened doors for me and allowed me to take on the challenges of the world with an excitement and boldness.

The Jam Pak community inspires me to be a good role model, friend, leader, listener, and human. This community has been a rock for me through high school, college, and now as a working adult. I believe that Jam Pak has shaped me as a person, as I am sure it has done with all that have been lucky enough to call Jam Pak family.

The lessons learned in Jam Pak are something that we carry with us every day. Jam Pak has made us better listeners and stronger speakers. Jam Pak has made us eager learners and quick studies. Jam Pak has taught us the power of music in making bridges and breaking down barriers. Jam Pak has taught us that much of our own strength comes from the strength of the community we surround ourselves with.

I hope that these lessons can be shared beyond Jam Pak and I hope that you as readers walk away with a new passion for building community.

Giselle Lee

Biology, Arizona State University, 2017
Instructor of Violin, Fiddle, Banjo
Music Maker Workshops
Fiddle/vocals Cisco & the Racecars

My Story

Photo by Patti Clemmer

I'm Anni Beach, founder and band leader of Jam Pak. I was almost 50 years old when my Rock and Hero, Vincent Beach, encouraged me to take out the mandolin my parents had brought from Italy some 25 years earlier. So, I decided to do it.

What a struggle! I wanted to give up but between my husband and my mother they just kept encouraging and helping me by practicing (flute and piano) with me. Now, I was 50 years old and that encouragement kept me going. I took that little instrument everywhere I went, as a substitute teacher, and played with children and got over some fears. Then Jam Pak was born on a sunny April day in 1994.

I'm now half way into the seventh decade of life. We sang my Rock and Hero Vincent on his way a few years ago. My small home is full of big love-wonderful people of all ages, crumbs and spills on the floor, every room full of instruments, antiques from my family, toys, photo albums of band and family history, and animals.

My caregivers are built-in. I have more social capitol than I can use in several lifetimes. My days are chocked full of music, details, gigs, and joy to the max.

There were days when I'd moan and carry on about, "What a lot of work!" And then some little person would, with intensity, pick out "Two Dollar Bill" on the banjo and my heart would soar. **YES!** Those few notes are my inspiration. And now in my old age, I have a super life. I've persevered!

The Beginning

Knock, knock, knock! There stood Lionel and CJ, two boys from the second-grade class I'd substituted in that day at Galveston Elementary, just a block up the street.

"Can we play more music?"

Photo by Vincent Beacn

I couldn't that day and this was something new to think about. I was 50 years old and a substitute teacher in Chandler, Arizona. I had been taking my mandolin to the schools so I could practice and play with the children.

I was determined to learn to play the mandolin and learn bluegrass music. I talked with my husband Vincent with the thought that maybe we should do something good for our neighborhood. Why not have a gathering each week and do some playing and singing with the children. He gave his full support.

The following week, Jam Pak was born with six neighbor children in our front yard. Armed only with harmonicas, songs, and my mandolin, we started something none of us could have imagined.

Who would have thought from such a simple beginning, would grow an Arizona State Banjo Champion, (and more on the way), multiple small bands, and thousands of people we've made happy with our music.

Who would have known that 6 and 7-year old children playing bluegrass would continue through college still serving as mentors to the younger waves of children joining Jam Pak.

What's This All About?

The question is often asked, "How do you carry out a music program in your home and keep it sustainable"?

Jam Pak was founded in our humble home nearly 25 years ago. We didn't set out to create a bluegrass children's band. We started out just sharing our love of music with neighborhood children. You could say we were on an accidental adventure that has turned into an amazing music mission.

Photo by Vincent Beach Jam Pak 1998

My husband Vincent Beach and I never could have imagined this journey. It's been a process of trial, error, success, and most of all **consistency** and **perseverance**.

5

From the first gathering of six little kids in our front yard singing "Tom Dooley", "The Circle Song", and blowing harmonicas, there was joy. This was a major crossroads—a beginning, really, in my life as the Jam Pak founder and leader. At first, Jam Pak was not multi-generational and the children met in our home once a week. Our first stringed instruments were homemade single-string fretted instruments called "Canjos". We began learning to sing traditional bluegrass and folk songs.

Jam Pak grew and flourished for many years. In 2012, our band experienced a death, but a fresh idea and passion followed. Debi Stone, one of our beloved band mothers, young and vibrant, died of brain cancer. Jam Pak members traveled to California to play for her service. The memorial service turned out to be truly inspiring.

Quietly, a challenge came forth from the minister. He talked about a study of 90-year olds who, when asked what they would have done differently in life, came up with three things they wished they would have done. They wished they would have *risked more, reflected more, and contributed more.*

In Jam Pak, we discussed these ideas including even our youngest members. A supporter of our band sent an idea after reading about Jam Pak: "*What if everyone who knows how to play an instrument teaches just one child, what a wonderful gift that would be.*"

Now there's a challenge! No one is so busy that it can't be done. The reasons we usually hear people give are: "I don't know enough." "I don't know how to work with kids." "I'm too busy." "Kids aren't interested." And from the older population, "I'm too old to learn to play."

We hope this Inspirational Guide will inspire you or someone you know to take the first small step. It may seem overwhelming to do what we've done for 25 years. The reality is that Jam Pak started with simple instruments and lots of commitment to take one step and then another.

This book is intended as a guide to a hugely fulfilling life if you love music and want to help others learn. Yes, there are risks but unfathomable rewards. We hope our reflections and contribution will give you the inspiration to create a home-based bluegrass music program. Small or big, **ENJOY!**

Lucy 3-

What Jam Pak means to me
is a great opportunity for me to
challenge myself into learning music.
Jam Pak is truly something I would
never ever quit because I have met
new friends over the past 6 years now
This is truly a life experience I will
never forget. ~~in my lifetime~~.

Why Bluegrass?

Bluegrass music reaches down deep. It's accessible with a few simple chords, easy tunes, portable, and is everyone's music. Folk music, old-time, and gospel music are usually included in the bluegrass genre.

From childhood through old age, it's music we can make together. Every country has strings and many countries have embraced this genre. It's sing-able and the words are understood and easily learned. The instruments are readily available from very inexpensive to the highest quality.

Photo by Alan Rodriguez

The main instruments for a bluegrass band are guitar, banjo, fiddle, mandolin, and bass. We add the washtub bass and mountain dulcimer to our mix.

Why the Home?

Home is where we usually are the most comfortable. We can teach, eat, store the things we need, and create a welcoming atmosphere. Schedules don't have to be coordinated with other facilities. No other facility has to be reimbursed for the space. The leader doesn't have to leave and go somewhere else to teach. And the refrigerator and stove are handy!

Photo by Anni Beach

Hospitality is a vital part of life. Gathering around a table, eating, talking, and sharing is a core value of family life. We believe that including this aspect in creating an atmosphere where band members feel that they belong is one of the reasons that keeps the band together year after year.

Band members learn to help prepare food, to serve each other, to clean up after their fun and food, and to feel so valued that someone cooks for them and has goodies available at every practice or event.

In the case of Jam Pak, the home is referred to as "our Jam Pak home". This creates respect for the surroundings and the fact that it belongs to all of us, creates that family feeling. Each person is encouraged by the leader and each other to remain part of the community-to make music and be happy with each other in this process.

Photo by Jenny DuFresne

The Jam Pak Philosophy

Photo by Debi Stone

From the beginning, the goal of Jam Pak has been to **"Make people and ourselves happy with our music."**

There are no auditions. The only requirement is that a member must be faithful to the band, attend, practice, and get along with everyone. No one individual is more important than the other *no matter how talented one might be*. Everyone is important in the band.

A philosophy has evolved over the years rather than written rules or regulations. I believe that the articles of the Jam Pak philosophy are what keeps Jam Pak thriving and making music now and in the years to come.

Everybody Learns

We stress an equal playing field in that even the coaches and every member and the leader are considered learners. **"Be hungry to improve"** is a motto that applies to *everyone* in the band.

Leadership

There is only one leader. This simplifies the process and keeps the band focused and growing. Leadership is modeled and taught in all that we do. Band members are given responsibilities at an early age to teach, to help others, to be part of the logistics of being on the road performing, to run small bands, and to be able to lead band practice. Band members sometimes comment: "Who's going to run Jam Pak when you die?" I remind them that they as band members are learning how to keep the band sustained for generations to come.

Community

We are building community at all times. Every birthday is celebrated. Photo albums are created which show the growth in this community. There are no written rules nor consequences with the types of manipulations that are part of a normal classroom environment. It's a music family. There are sad times when a member must be excused from further participation as their actions are detrimental to the band. The band itself is an entity which must be preserved over the individual.

Photo by Jenny DuFresne

Fun and joy must be built into the time together. Laughing, talking, playing games, drawing, toys, special outings to a park, creating a soccer game, movie night, potlucks, cooking, and making music with a light spirit. We aren't trying to reach Carnegie Hall. We want the joy of making music together.

Diversity is the spice of life. We consciously bring people together from various nationalities as well as cultures and economic conditions. Growing up like this creates lifelong friendships and the ability to relate easily to many kinds of people.

Participation is critical to any band. Band members get to play and perform no matter how far along they are in learning. This gives each person courage and confidence to keep getting better.

Each One Teach One is a necessity of Jam Pak. We have only volunteers and the adult coaches are limited in how often they can teach. So as band members learn how to do something, that knowledge is passed on to other members. It's truly amazing to see the teaching that goes on from person to person, young or older alike. This is one of our best accomplishments and it mirrors how this music has survived from generation to generation.

Celebrations include a birthday party for every member-that's a cake, a gathering around the cake, singing, and I, as band leader, give a speech about the birthday person. Photos are taken. Graduations are celebrated. Parties are a must for this band. The band members plan special occasion parties, and there is a yearly Christmas party with a gift exchange. The Gingerbread House contest is now held yearly at one of our Jam Pak friends' home. Dance parties are especially fun times. Traditions are maintained.

Kindness in the smallest things like helping a band member tune the instrument, to helping with homework, to giving compliments, to bringing clothing and food to share, to building up and never tearing down, to serving food, and to sharing personal stories. In Jam Pak, kindness is a daily act.

Caring and kindness go hand in hand but caring goes a little further in seeing when someone is hurting and finding out why and giving comfort. We have two young people who serve as Camp Mom and Dad and are responsible for personal appearance, treating minor wounds and illness, getting members seated whether in practice or on the road and attempting to make everyone comfortable.

Photo by Rusty Childress

Guidance is hopefully given in a common-sense way. "Treat each other as you would want to be treated." Acceptance is such a big part of giving guidance or counsel. Having band members of all ages gives a unique opportunity for the older band members to help children navigate growing up. The band leader must be sensitive to the variety of issues that children can be dealing with and try to help them find solutions. The very practical side of guidance is that band members stay playing music!

Love is in all that we do. We love to make music. We love to be together with our friends. We have a sense of purpose in making ourselves and people happy with our music. We accept each other as unique individuals and as worthy of love and joyful lives. We try to do all things with love whether learning a new song, washing up the dishes, or feeding the animals.

Adventure means an extension of fun. "Let's go to California!" Many years ago we took our first trip to San Diego in the old motor home based on that comment from a young member. We broke down, kept going, saw the ocean for the first time, got buried in the sand, and have the photos to prove all the years of traveling to new places.

Photo by Mike Headrick

Patience is perhaps the hardest attribute to maintain in the midst of a large group of band members, making noise, talking, not picking up after themselves, or not doing what they've been asked to do. Yet, to have a group of people who want to stay together, make music, have joy, the band leader needs to develop a super abundance of patience. This does not translate to a lack of direction or control, but it is a mindset and inner calm that must be developed and modeled. Everyone does not progress at the same rate. For some it takes years to become proficient. **But the bottom line is to enjoy making music with others and for that to be a lifetime skill and experience.**

Keep It Simple must read like, "You've got to be kidding!" after all the above statements. But this is just life and it unfolds as you go along. You meet, you greet, you learn music, you eat, have fun, love one another, and you go and perform. Everything falls into place. It's work, *real work*, but it can be simple.

The Leader Philosophy

Most of us are called on to be leaders at some point in our lives and there are some basic principles which apply to nearly every situation. To be an effective leader, one needs to be inclusive in decision-making and yet still maintain the over-all well-being of the organization.

In the case of leading the band of all ages, I believe that the playing field is equal. Everyone is expected to respect each other regardless of age. Being fair to all members and letting each member know how important they are to the well-being of the band is

vital. There can be no gossip between the leader and parents or other band members. Confidences must be kept.

Vincent Beach had a saying, "Dirt won't kill you unless it falls on you." Or it might be said a little mess won't hurt you when there are spills or breakage. **Calmness** in the face of pressures such as performing, losing picks, or one more trip to pick up a member who can't get to practice without your transport, is vital. Easy to do? No, but experience shows that these things are nothing compared to creating beautiful bluegrass music with a unified band of all ages.

A leader must be able to say, "I'm sorry." It's so easy to yell or get mad in the frustrations of a lot of activity going on in a small space or a child not doing what you've asked of them. As Maya Angelou so eloquently said, "I've learned that people will forget what you said, people will forget what you did, but people will never forget how you made them feel." A leader must have humility and be able to apologize when they've been hasty in some judgment or have been harsh in their words and actions.

A leader, above all, needs to keep their word, be gentle in corrections, have respect for every person, persevere, and be the model of what they expect of the band members.

Embrace the process! Have a welcoming spirit!
Enjoy!

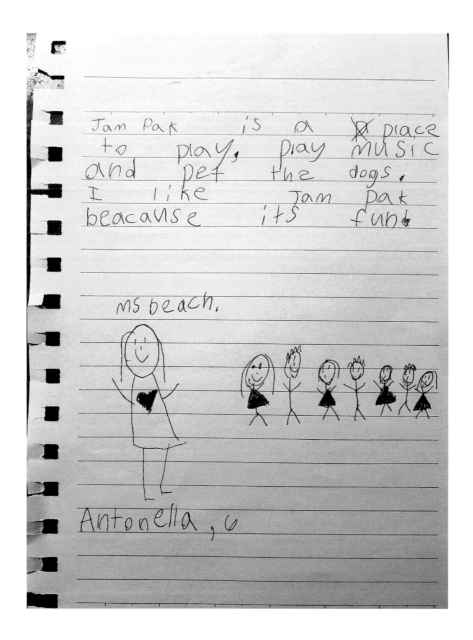

Jam Pak is a place to play, play music and pet the dogs. I like Jam Pak beacause its fun.

ms beach.

Antonella, 6

What Jampak means
to me is we make
everybody happy with our
music.Jampak truly makes
me happy.

One Way to Get Started

Keep it very simple.

You could share a statement like this with people you know: **"I'm wanting to have a bluegrass gathering each week here in my home. We'll learn together. You can try different instruments. We'll learn some songs. Come and see what you think."**

Start with whatever instruments you have. If you only have guitars or banjos, start with those. Use what you have!

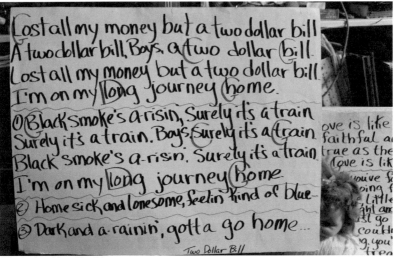

Photo by Alan Rodriguez

Have three songs on poster board with the lyrics and the chords. Singing is the most essential part of the learning. Keep it to about an hour. It's NOT school or a classroom environment. The atmosphere needs to be relaxed and yet purposeful. Have snacks and drinks.

You might start with your own family and then include their friends. Create a welcoming atmosphere. There are things to look at, to play with, and instruments are readily available.

One adult leads with patience and an inclusive spirit. **"We're all learning and I'll do my best to help and we'll help each other."**

Once members learn to pick a tune they are usually hooked. Your leadership is to encourage, persevere, and keep in touch. Call on the phone before practice and remind. Use Facebook or whatever social media the children and adults use to keep in touch.

In Jam Pak, the children are responsible to the band and for being in the band so the contacts need to be leader to children. Adults also need to be updated and reminded either by personal calls or e-mail. The personal call is never out of date. The leader must reach out, communicate, and **LOVE THE PROCESS**. The social nature of the music itself is what attracts and holds by creating the feeling of belonging.

Progress After the Start-up

Hold a house concert every few months. The band members demonstrate what they've learned and can talk about the songs. Parents and friends come and see just what is happening and can see the progress and joy in the music.

Pick a name for your group. I created the name (Jam Pak) before the first gathering. The rest of the name was added when we really sounded like a band! Eventually design a logo and make tee shirts. All costs must be kept low. **Jam Pak is free**. Often people don't start anything because they feel they must have financial backing or be a non-profit and so nothing much gets off the ground.

It's great to have someone video the singing and playing and show it back to the band. The band members love it. It gives us encouragement of what can be improved and what's good. We watch the video and look for what can be better such as reminding how to use the mics for the best sound. "And please don't yawn or scratch when we're on stage." We want to do the best we can so the critique is not ever meant to make someone feel bad or embarrassed. We are all learning. Band members volunteer to help another member who is having difficulty saying some words or playing a break so that no one is left stranded.

Eventually, it's great to begin performing publicly in nursing homes, children's events, church, or jamming in the park. There need to be goals to reach and performing is a great motivator. It is important to remember that this is NOT about perfection. It is about getting started and for the band to gain experience. If there is a note or two missed, it is a good time to remember this is part of the learning process. *Don't worry.*

Just get going. People will help. My guiding philosophy is, **"I'll be faithful to what's been given to me to do, and we'll have what we need."** And that philosophy has worked for 25-years.

7 Core Bluegrass Songs

Jam Pak has seven core songs that everyone works towards playing and singing. Trophies are awarded at special celebrations once a year. Seven traditional bluegrass tunes were chosen many years ago by bluegrass leaders in Arizona so that beginners would have a core list of songs they could play with other "pickers".

- Ol' Joe Clark - Key of A
- I Saw the Light - Key of G
- Meet Me on the Mountain (Say, Won't You Be Mine) - Key of G
- I'm On My Way Back to the Old Home - Key of G
- Your Love is Like a Flower - Key of G
- Boil That Cabbage Down - Key of A or G
- Two Dollar Bill - Key of G

Jam Pak members are expected to be able to play and sing these songs by memory and be able to take a short "break" (solo) on their instrument.

Jam Pak is a fun place to play my insterment and I love all the music and people that are here and we get to go on camping trips and I get to learn a lot of new, fun and beautiful songs.

Mikaela

7 Bluegrass Skills

Jam Pak developed a list of seven bluegrass skills that are needed to become a bluegrass musician and to earn the Bluegrass Skills Trophy.

1. Be able to play scales in the keys of C, G, D, A for fiddle, guitar, mandolin, dulcimer, and bass.
   a. Banjo: Be able to play forward rolls, backward rolls, alternating thumb rolls
   b. Banjo: Be able to read and follow tablature

2. Demonstrate the I, IV, V and relative minor chords for the keys of C, G, D, A-- All instruments and how to use a capo as needed.

3. Be able to improvise a break for a bluegrass tune.

4. Demonstrate jam signals during a jam for (1) a turnaround, (2) stop (3) passing the break, (4) calling the key

5. Be able to do rhythm back-up and change chords at proper time.

6. Know how to tune to another instrument or tuning machine.

7. Keep a working notebook of bluegrass tunes and lyrics and be able to describe what traditional bluegrass music is, who formed the tradition, and what instruments are generally acceptable.

An Afternoon at Jam Pak

The band leader is at the house to greet everyone and help them get started with their practicing, snacking, or relaxing a bit after school.

Snacks and water are already on the table. The early birds set up the room for practice. I use folding chairs and as the living room is quite small, I don't have large furniture. The band members get their instruments ready. Some bring instruments with them, while others have their special ones at the house. They get tuned. They practice with each other. After everyone arrives the whole group works on songs using the charts of words and chords. We work for 45 minutes to an hour on several songs that are being prepared for performance.

After working on Jam Pak songs, we break into smaller organized bands which are youth-led. We also have lessons once a week to work on the individual instruments. Everyone is expected to either give a lesson or receive a lesson. We have a few volunteer adult coaches who come in to teach specific instruments or band coaching. As Jam Pak meets twice a week, this schedule is a good one. Once a week to gather and practice and create a band is essential for real progress to be made.

At the end of practices, the group comes back together, and we have food. The band members socialize and may do homework or play games with each other. Parents then pick up the younger members or they are driven home by an available driver.

In our case, the schedule is loose. Band members may stay a long time and work on other music, help each other with homework, and visit. The younger ones like to play games and "family". All of this activity is part of creating "community" and keeping the music alive and thriving.

Inclusive Thoughts

Our band, Jam Pak Blues 'N' Grass Neighborhood Band, is a neighborhood band. Our neighborhood happens to be in a racially diverse area and so the band has always been inclusive and reflective of a wide population. We consciously seek to present bluegrass as *"everyone's music."* The friendships made are lifelong and music is at the core of this Jam Pak community.

Photo by Mike Headrick

People need the association of people outside their own culture and bluegrass music is a great way to achieve this. You may need to reach out to people in a nearby school or church and purposely seek folks of a different background. It's a long process but with love and perseverance, lives are changed. Beautiful music is created, skills of teamwork, social know-how, leadership, confidence, empathy, and character are developed.

What jam pak means to me?

Jam Pak isn't just some place I go too meet up with friends and play music. Jam Pak is where I go when I see my second family. It's more to me then just a group of friends there my rock. Jam Pak has brought me many expriences that I cant experience anywhere. Jam Pak is my everything and I love them all to death Is more than music it's family.

Sincerly: Alasya Zenella

Puberty

Here's the part that families may somewhat dread. The little children in the band begin to develop interests outside of the family. Perhaps years have been spent developing a young musician. And suddenly sports, sexuality issues, school clubs, and dating become prime interest, and the questioning of one's abilities and attractiveness.

Photo by Fran Denoncourt

What do we do to hold our musicians together and continue to make music? We cannot, as leaders, fight this natural period of life nor gossip about it to others.

Acceptance and grace of the changes is paramount. Being a person that band members can tell anything to is vital. The leader needs to always be in the band member's corner, as a guide and mentor, but the members are responsible for their choices and their music. Calm and reassuring guidance is most always welcomed by young band members.

The band member must be responsible for their own participation and actions. Stressing that they are working and learning as brothers and sisters, and respect for each other is of the utmost concern. This is a band family and for some *just plain family*.

Photo by Rusty Childress

We never change from Tuesday and Thursday practices, but during some sports seasons the band members may come just once a week or come after sports practice. This is not easy to do and may require extra transportation.

We always have several members in Student Council at their schools or in various clubs and sports and music. And for some, sports takes the leading role and they simply can't do the music at this time of their life. But if at all possible, we work around it. This is a multi-generational band and the experienced young people are the leaders of today, tomorrow, and for the sustainability of Jam Pak.

What Jam Pak means to me!

Jam pak, is a band where you can express your emotions with music and feel comfortable. Everyone is excepted and are treated with respect and.

Sasha

Jam pak is my best frm
this bland in my honw
becnuse whll I wns a
Litllgln I won't to play
and I what ts al s meins

Why Jam Pak Works

The question was posed to young members and those who have grown up in Jam Pak for many years: **Why do you stay in Jam Pak? What keeps you here year after year? Here are the answers to that question.**

> *"Our friends are here and we support each other. We feel like we belong somewhere and are doing something important. It's free. You take care of us. We are accepted by everyone. We get to learn something new and have something to look forward to each week. We learn about ourselves. I get to do what I enjoy. We can come and practice at any time because it's in your home. We have fun together. We all love each other. Our friends and sisters and brothers are also here and that makes it cool. We learn to make music and that is a way of life for us. It's amazing to have people all love what we do. We get respect from so many people. We get to travel and camp and be part of festivals. We get new experiences."*

Jam Pak seeks to imitate the roots of the music. It's not a competition nor a solo kind of music.

Bluegrass is sometimes called "down home music", "back porch music", or "roots music". And in our case it's really **"Living Room Music!"**

It's something we do for enjoyment with our family and neighbors- playing and singing together just for fun or to entertain others.

The learning, fun, joy, and belonging are limitless. I hope this book can be a do-able framework on which to launch your own music mission-whatever the size or scope.

Put Your Own Thumbprint on It

Jam Pak is a band with a unique mission: Make people and ourselves happy with music.

It took us years to develop much of what you have read here.

Music and creating a band is a unique experience.

The most important thing about creating a band that makes people happy with its music is to put your own thumbprint on it.

What does JamPak mean to me?

A simple, yet complex question; to others, Jam Pak would only be seen as an "extra cirricular" activity, or "something to do when I'm bored." Wrong, very wrong, actually. Jam Pak is a place where everyone is embraced and recognized, a place for everyone to feel like they belong, and that is the best way to explain my feelings about Jam Pak. I have never felt like I belonged somewhere more than I have in Jam Pak. I have met some of the best people here, in which I've made unbreakable connections and everlasting bonds. And not to mention the music. So much music, everywhere, by everyone; the young, old, the black, the white, the experienced, and the rookies, everyone is unified through a passion for music, people, and happiness. And what's not to love about that?

Selena Haggerty Tavera 17

What does Jam Pak mean to me?

Jam Pak is the one place where I can be myself, it is filled with so many different kinds of people. Jam Pak is my second family, it is so much more than just meeting up with friends at a place, the music connects us all. We all put our blood and tears in our music. Jam Pak is my home, nothing can ever change that.

-Rosy ♡

What does Jam Pak mean to me?

Jam Pak to me is not only a place to make music but a place to make friends and laugh. I get out of school excited to go to Jam Pak. I love to sing with the people in Jam Pak. I call them my family. I love them so much and nothing can change that.

— Nazarena Delgado

What does JamPak Mean to Me?

To me, JamPak is a place that you can make others happy with music. Not because someone is making you, but because you want to. This is a place where you can grow as an individual, and better yourself. No matter how good you are, you can always get better. JamPak is a place where you can pass on what you learned, or what know to the next JamPak generation. We are always growing in people but that's ok, it just means more heads to learn. I'm excited to see what new things I can learn from JamPak!

- Alan Moreno
. am

47

What does Jam Pak mean to me?

Jam Pak has given me the opportunity to Express myself. It has also given me the opportunity to help others with music and Life in general. I've been in jampak 16 years now and it's been one of my most cherishable Experiences. That continues to grow. We all grow together and learn from eachother in Jampak. Yes, every rose has its thorns but this rose allows everyone to bloom. In the future I want to work with Kids and open an LGBT youth Center. ~~That~~ ~~to work with Kids and better myself.~~ Not only has jampak allowed me to work ~~with~~ with Kids, but its helped me futher myself and get a taste of what my future is going to be like and boy its bright! Thanks JamPak!

-Justin Mzer

Jampak is my best band because I have alot of friend in jampak and I love ms. Beach and she is a very nice person and I like ms. Beach's music

Jam Pak What it means it to me...

Jam pak means to me...that Jam pak is a hard-working and fun please to be at and it's not a place to put neglitive stuff to say too other peoples smiles down so that all I have to say. love Aláine

Made in the USA
Columbia, SC
15 February 2024